FM 23-5 REPRINT

M1 Garand
Rifle Caliber .30

(Department of the Army – May 1965)

MIDDLE
COAST
PUBLISHING

Middle-Coast-Publishing.com

FM 23-5 REPRINT
M1 Garand

Rifle Caliber .30

ISBN-978-0934523-09-7

Editor@Middle-Coast-Publishing.com

CONTENTS

Dedicated to the genius that was John Garand.

Jean (John) Cantius Garand demonstrating how to load his brainchild, the M1 Garand, with an en bloc clip.

Chapter 1.

INTRODUCTION

1. Purpose and Scope

(a) This manual is a guide for commanders and instructors in presenting instruction and training in the mechanical operation of the M1 rifle. It includes a detailed description of the rifle and its general characteristics; procedures for disassembly and assembly; methods of loading; an explanation of functioning; a discussion of stoppages and immediate action; a description of the ammunition; and instructions on the care and cleaning of both the weapon and ammunition. The material presented is applicable, without modification, to both nuclear and non-nuclear warfare.

(b) Marksmanship training is covered in FM 23-71.

(c) Users of this manual are encouraged to submit recommended changes or comments to improve the manual. Comments should be keyed to the specific page, paragraph, and line of the text in which the change is recommended. Reasons should be provided for each comment to insure understanding and complete evaluation. Comments should be forwarded direct to the Commandant, U.S. Army Infantry School, Fort Benning, Georgia.

2. Importance of Mechanical Training

The rifle is the soldier's basic weapon. It gives him an individual and powerful capability for combat. To get the most out of his individual combat capability, the soldier must develop two skills to an equal degree: he must be able to fire his weapon well enough to get hits on battlefield targets, and he must know enough about its working parts to keep them operating smoothly so the rifle will not fail him. The soldier gets his firing skill on marksmanship training ranges and he learns how to keep his rifle in firing condition from the mechanical training that is outlined in this manual.

3. Description of the Rifle

The U.S. rifle caliber .30, M1, (fig. 1) is an air-cooled, gas-operated, clip-fed, and semiautomatic shoulder weapon. This means that the air cools the barrel; that the power to cock the rifle and chamber the succeeding round comes from the expanding gas of the round fired previously; that it is loaded by inserting a metal clip (containing a maximum of eight rounds) into the receiver; and that the rifle fires one round each time the trigger is pulled.

Table I

General Data	(Specifications)
Weight	9.5 pounds
Weight w/bayonet M1 and sling M1907	11.2 pounds
Length: (over-all) rifle only	43.6 inches
Length (over-all) with bayonet M1	53.4 inches
Length of barrel	24 inches
Length of rifling	70.8 calibers (21.30 inches)
Rifling, old barrels	Four grooves
Rifling, new barrels	Two grooves
Rifling twist	Right hand, one turn in 33.3 calibers (one in 10 inches)
Depth of grooves, rifling	0.0040 inches
Type of mechanism	Gas operated, semi-automatic
Loading device	En-block clip
Sight radius	27.9 inches at 100 yard range
Sights: Front	Fixed blade
Sights: Rear	Adjustable peep. One click of elevation or windage moves the strike of the bullet .7 centimeters at 25 meters
Trigger pull: Minimum	5 ½ pounds
Trigger pull: Maximum	7 ½ pounds
Ammunition types	Ball, AP, tracer, grenade - See Chapter 6.
Muzzle velocity (M-2 ammunition)	853 (2,800 fps) meters/sec
Chamber pressure	50,000 pounds per square inch (copper)
Maximum range	3,200 meters (3,450 yards)
Maximum effective range	460 meters.
Maximum effective rate of fire	16 to 24 rounds per minute. A trained rifleman fires 16 to 24 aimed rounds per minute)

Chapter 2.

MECHANICAL TRAINING

5. Disassembly and Assembly

(a.) The individual soldier is authorized to disassemble his rifle to the extent called field stripping.

(b.) The rifle should be disassembled and assembled only when maintenance is required or for

instructional purposes. Repeated disassembly and assembly causes excessive wear of parts and soon makes them unserviceable and reduces the accuracy of the weapon.

(c.) The rifle has been designed so that it may be taken apart and put together easily. No force is needed if it is disassembled and assembled correctly. The parts of one rifle, except the bolt, may be interchanged with those of another when necessary; for safety reasons, bolts should never be interchanged except by maintenance support personnel.

(d.) As the rifle is disassembled, the parts should be laid out on a clean surface, in the order of removal, from left to right. This makes assembly easier because the parts are assembled in the reverse order of disassembly. The names of the rifle parts (nomenclature) should be taught along with disassembly and assembly to make future instruction on the rifle easier to understand.

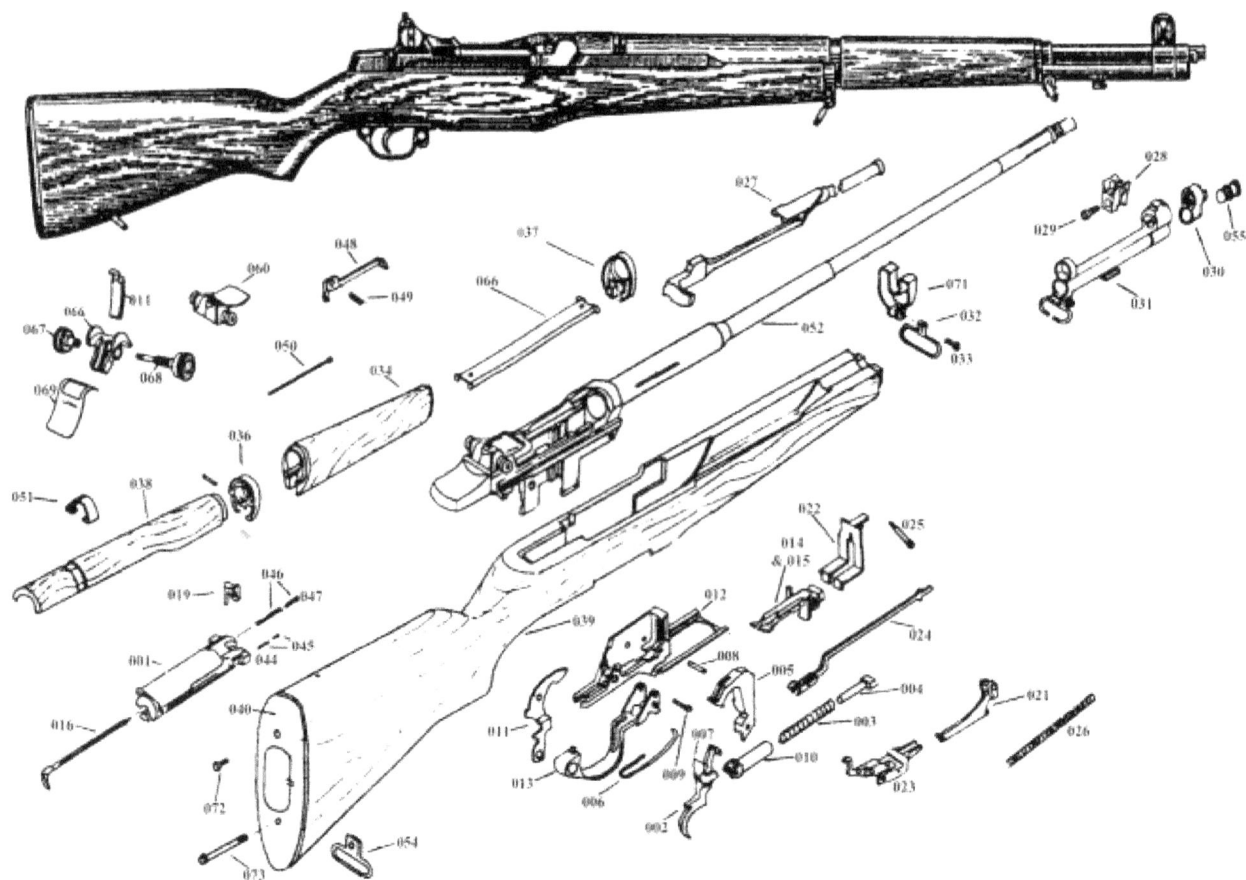

Exploded view: U.S. Rifle, Cal. .30 M1

6. Clearing the Rifle

The first step in handling any weapon is to clear it. If the rifle is loaded, unload it as described in paragraph 13. The M1 rifle is clear when there is no ammunition in the chamber or receiver, the bolt is locked to the rear, and the safety is engaged. To clear the rifle, pull the operating rod handle all the way to the rear, inspect the chamber and receiver to insure that no rounds are present and push the safety to its locked position (inside the trigger guard).

7. Disassembly Into the Three Main Groups

(a.) The three main groups are the trigger housing group, the barrel and receiver group, and the stock group.

(b.) To disassemble the rifle into the three main groups, first insure that the weapon is clear and then allow the bolt to go forward by depressing the follower with the right thumb and allowing the bolt to ride forward over the follower assembly.

(c.) Place the rifle butt against the left thigh, sights to the left. With the thumb and forefinger of the right hand, pull downward and outward on the rear of the trigger guard. Swing the trigger guard out as far as it will go and lift out the trigger housing group.

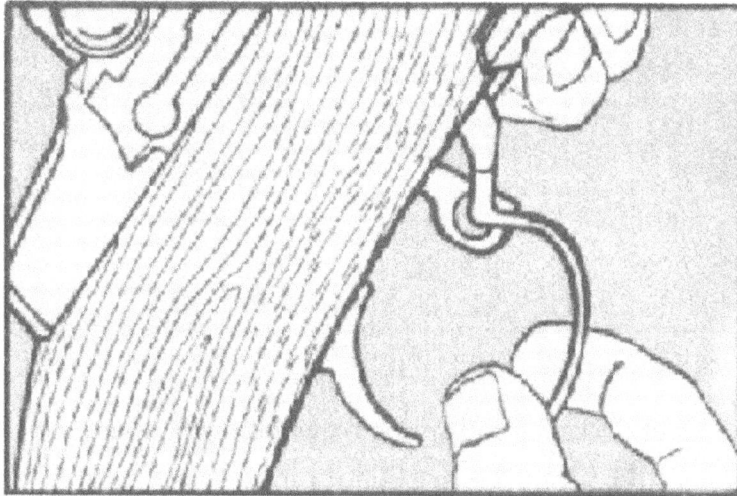

(d.) To separate the barrel and receiver from the stock lay the weapon on a flat surface with the sights up, muzzle to the left. With the left hand, grasp the rear of the receiver and raise the rifle. With the right hand, give a downward blow, grasping the small of the stock. This will separate the stock group from the barrel and receiver group.

8. Disassembly of the Barrel and Receiver Group

(a.) Place the barrel and receiver group, with the bolt closed, on a flat surface with the sights down (insuring that the rear sight aperture is at its lowest position), muzzle pointing to the left. Holding the rear of the receiver with the right hand, grasp the follower rod with the thumb and forefinger of the left hand and disengage it from the follower arm by moving it toward the muzzle

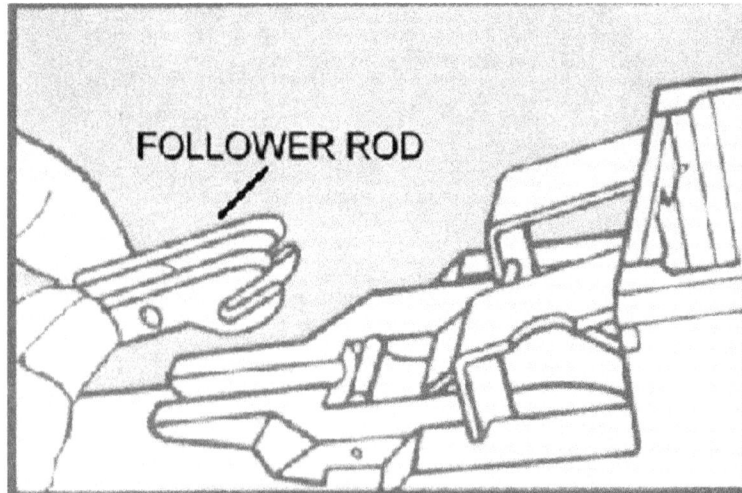

FOLLOWER ROD

Remove the follower rod and operating rod spring by withdrawing them to the right. Do not separate these parts.

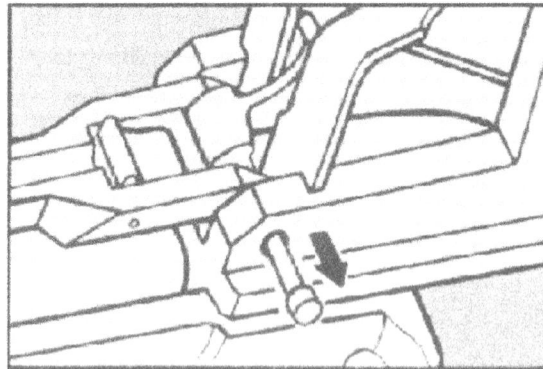

(b.) Using the tip of a dummy cartridge, remove the follower arm pin by pushing it from the far side of the receiver toward the body.

   (c.) With the left hand, grasp the bullet guide, follower arm, and the operating rod catch assembly, and lift them out of the receiver together.

Separate and arrange these parts from left to right in the following order: follower arm, operating rod catch assembly, and bullet guide.

(d.) Reach down into the receiver and lift out the follower assembly.

(e.) Turn the barrel and receiver group over so that the sights are up, muzzle pointing away from you. With the left hand, raise the rear of the receiver. With the right hand, pull the operating rod to the rear until the rear of the handle is directly under the forward edge of the windage knob. With an upward and outward movement, disengage the guide lug of the operating rod through its dismount notch on the receiver. Remove the operating rod.

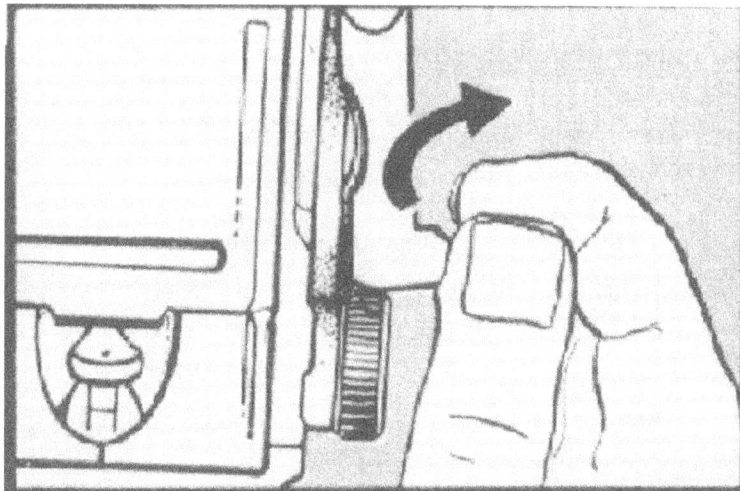

Caution: The operating rod is bent intentionally so that it will not bind against the enlarged portion of the barrel. Do not attempt to straighten it.

(f.) With the right hand, grasp the bolt by the operating lug and slide it fully to the rear; then slide it forward, lifting upward and outward to the right front with a slight rotating motion to remove it.

(g.) Using the screwdriver blade of the M10 cleaning rod handle unscrew and remove the gas cylinder lock screw located under the end of the barrel muzzle,

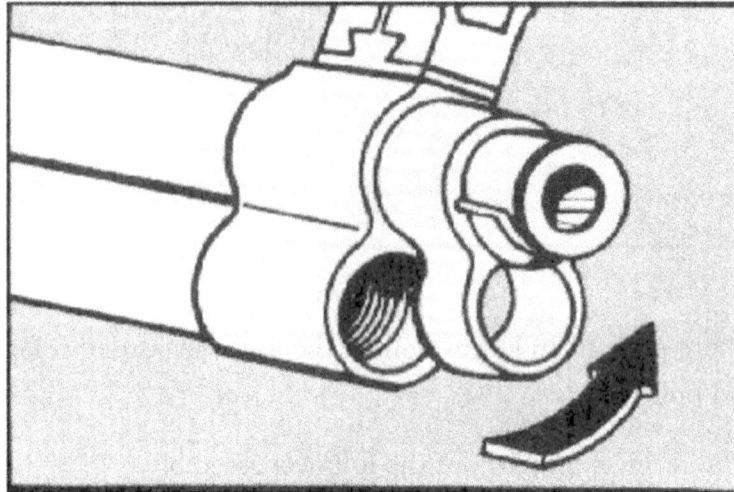

(h.) Unscrew and remove the gas cylinder lock. Loosen the gas cylinder by tapping lightly toward the muzzle on the bayonet stud with a piece of wood or similar soft object. Remove the gas cylinder, taking care not to burr or damage the splines. Do not remove or attempt to adjust the front sight.

(i.) Remove the front handguard by sliding it forward over the muzzle. Do not attempt to remove the rear handguard.

9. Assembly of the Barrel and Receiver Group

(a.) Replace the front handguard by sliding it over the muzzle and insure that it is seated in the front band.

(b.) Place the gas cylinder over the barrel, making sure the splines are aligned with their grooves. Push the gas cylinder down as far as it will go. If tapping is necessary, use a piece of wood on the bayonet stud. Engage the threads of the gas cylinder lock with those on the barrel and screw the lock on by hand until it is finger tight (do not use a tool). If the lock is not aligned with the gas cylinder, do not force it, but unscrew it until it is aligned. Replace and tighten the gas cylinder lock screw with the handle assembly of the M10 cleaning rod.

(c.) To replace the bolt, hold it by the operating lug and place the rear end of the bolt onto the bridge of the receiver. Rotate the bolt counter-clockwise as far as necessary to permit the tang of the firing pin to clear the top of the bridge of the receiver. Guide the left locking lug of the bolt into its groove on the left side of the receiver. Lower the right locking lug on its bearing surface and slide the bolt halfway to the rear.

(d.) To replace the operating rod, hold the handle with the right hand and place the piston end into the gas cylinder. Align the operating rod so that the recess in the hump fits over the operating lug of the bolt. While applying pressure downward and inward on the handle, pull the operating rod to the rear until the guide lug is engaged in its groove. Move the operating rod forward until the bolt is closed.

(e.) Turn the barrel and receiver group over so that the sights are down and the muzzle is to the left. Replace the follower assembly so that its guide ribs fit into their grooves in the receiver. Make sure that the slide of the follower is down and that the square hole is to the rear. The slide will rest against the bolt.

(f.) Replace the bullet guide so that its shoulders fit into their slots in the receiver and the hole in the toe of the bullet guide is aligned with the holes in the receiver.

(g.) With the right hand, lift up the lower part of the bullet guide slightly. With the left hand, insert the rear arm of the operating rod catch assembly through the clearance cut in the side of the bullet guide. Make sure that the rear arm is underneath the front stud of the clip latch which projects into the receiver. Lower the bullet guide into place. Test for correct assembly by pressing down on the front arms of the operating rod catch assembly. It should move and you should be able to feel the tension of the clip latch spring.

(h.) Replace the follower arm by passing its rear studs through the bullet guide and inserting them into the guide grooves on the follower. Allow the wings of the follower arm to rest astride the toe of the bullet guide. Align the holes in the operating rod catch assembly, follower arm, and bullet guide with those in the receiver and replace the follower arm pin from the near side.

(i.) Insert the loose end of the operating rod spring into the operating rod. Grasp the follower rod with the left hand, making sure that its hump is toward the barrel. Pull toward the muzzle, compressing the operating rod spring, and engage the claws of the follower rod with the front studs of the follower arm. You may have to raise the follower assembly to do this.

10. Assembly of the Three Main Groups

(a.) Place the barrel and receiver group on a flat surface, sights down. Pick up the stock group and engage the U-shaped flange of the stock ferrule in the lower band, then lower the stock group onto the barrel and receiver group.

(b.) Unlatch and open the trigger guard. Keeping the base of the trigger housing group level, place it straight down into the receiver, making sure that the locking lugs on the trigger guard enter their recesses in the receiver. Place the butt of the rifle on the left thigh with the sights to the left. Close the trigger guard and latch it by striking it with the heel of the right hand. The trigger guard is latched while the rifle is in this position so that the rear sight will not be damaged.

11. Test for Correct Assembly

Each time the rifle is disassembled and assembled it should be tested to make sure that it is put together properly. To do this, pull the operating rod to its rearmost position. The bolt should stay open. Close the bolt and snap the safety to its locked position. Squeeze the trigger. The hammer should not fall. Push the safety to its unlocked position and squeeze the trigger. The hammer should fall. This test is made to check the operation of the safety.

Chapter 3.

OPERATION AND FUNCTIONING

12. Loading the Rifle

(a.) Single round. To load a single round, pull the operating rod all the way to the rear. While holding the muzzle below the horizontal, place a round in the chamber an seat it with the thumb. With a knife edge of the right hand against the operating rod handle, force the operating rod slightly to the rear. Push down on the follower assembly with the right thumb and allow the bolt to ride forward. Remove the thumb from the follower assembly and release the operating rod handle, allowing the operating rod to go all the way forward.

(b.) Full clip. To load a full clip, hold the rifle at the balance with the left hand and pull the operating rod handle all the way to the rear. Place the butt of the rifle against the thigh or on the ground. With the right hand, place a full clip on top of the follower assembly. Place the thumb on the center of the top round in the clip and press the clip straight down into the receiver until it catches. Swing the right hand up and to the right to clear the bolt in its forward movement. Note that the operating rod is not held to the rear during loading since there is no danger of it going forward as long as pressure is maintained on the top round in the clip. It may be necessary to strike forward on the operating rod handle with the heel of the right hand to fully close and lock the bolt.

(c.) Partially filled clip. To load a partially filled clip, hold the rifle in the same manner prescribed for a full clip. With the operating rod all the way to the rear, place an empty clip into the receiver. Place the first round into the clip and on the follower, to the left of the follower slide. Press the second round into the clip, exerting a downward, turning motion until the round snaps into place. Load the remaining rounds in the same manner. With the knife edge of the the right hand against the operating rod handle force the operating rod slightly to the rear. Push down on the top round with the right thumb, allowing the bolt to start the top round forward. Remove the right hand and allow the operating rod to go forward.

13. Unloading the Rifle

(a.) To unload a round from the chamber, support the rifle butt on the thigh or on the ground; with the right hand grasp the operating rod handle and pull the operating rod slowly to the rear. At the same time, place the left hand, palm down, over the receiver to catch the round as it is ejected. This keeps the round from falling into the dirt or away from your position.

(b.) To unload a filled or partially filled clip, unload the round that is in the chamber as described in (a.) above. When the operating rod reaches its rearmost position, hold it there. Place the palm of the left hand over the receiver and depress the clip latch with the left thumb, allowing the clip to be ejected up into the hand, Do not relax the rearward pressure on the operating rod handle until after the clip has been removed.

14. Loading Rounds into a Clip

(a.) Insert eight rounds into the clip, holding the clip, open end upward, and the rounds in palm of your left hand. Start placing the rounds in from the lower left of the clip and make sure that each round is against the rear wall so that the inner rib of the clip engages the extracting groove of each round. The top round will then be on the right, making the clip easier for a right handed firer to load in the rifle. For the same reason, clips are loaded this way at arsenals.

(b.) Each time rounds are loaded into a clip, the clip should be checked for long rounds. If one rounds extends beyond the others, it will be hard to load the clip into the rifle. The long round should be seated by removing the top round, pushing the long round into place and then replacing the top round. Tapping the bullet against a solid surface to seat the long round may result in the bullet being pushed back into its cartridge case. This may damage the bullet or break the bullet seal which could result in changes in the ballistic performance of the round.

15. Functioning of the Rifle

(a.) The trigger must be pulled to fire each round. When the last round is fired, the empty clip is automatically ejected and the bolt remains to the rear.

(b.) Each time a round is loaded and fired, many parts inside the rifle work in a given order. This is known as the cycle of operation. This cycle is similar in all small arms. A knowledge of what happens inside the rifle during this cycle of operation will help the soldier understand the cause of and remedy for various stoppages.

(c.) The cycle of operations is broken down into eight steps. These steps are listed below, together with a brief description of what actually occurs inside the rifle during each step. Assume that a full or partially filled clip has been loaded into the rifle and that the first round has been fired and the bolt is in its rearmost position.

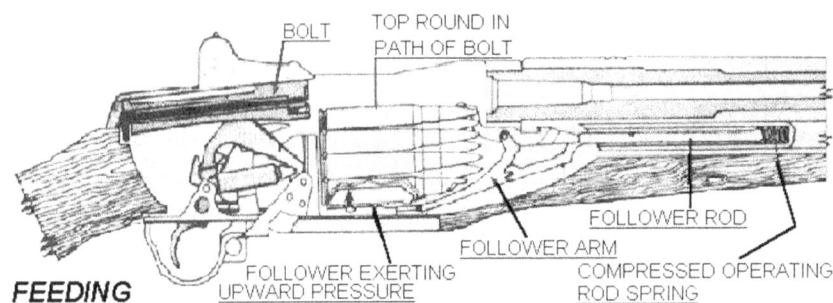

Cycle of Operation

(1.) Feeding. Feeding takes place when a round is moved into the path of the bolt. This is done by the follower assembly exerting an upward pressure on the bottom round in the clip. The follower assembly is continuously forced up by the pressure of the operating rod spring through the follower rod and the follower arm (fig. 24).

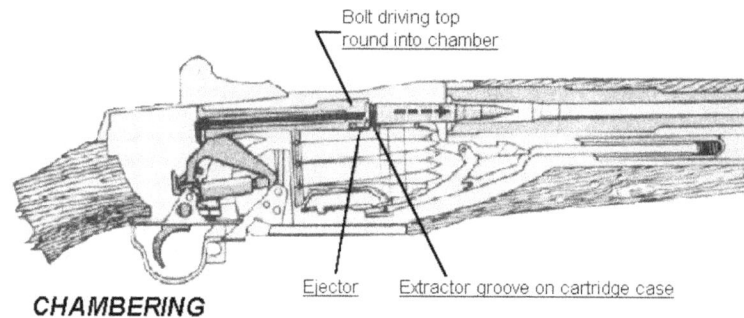

CHAMBERING

Chambering

(2.) Chambering occurs when a round is moved into the chamber. This takes place as the bolt goes forward under pressure of the expanding operating rod spring, picking up the top round in the clip and driving it forward into the chamber (fig. 25). Chambering is complete when the extractor snaps into the extracting groove on the cartridge case and the ejector is forced into the face of the bolt.

(3.) Locking. Locking is complete when the bolt is fully closed. This prevents the loss of gas pressure until the bullet has left the muzzle. The bolt is locked by the rear camming surface in the recess in the hump of the operating rod, forcing the operating lug of the bolt down. This engages the locking lugs on the bolt with their recesses in the receiver (fig. 26).

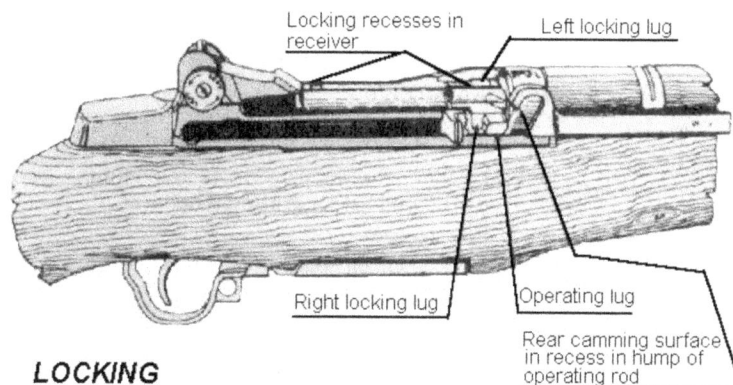

LOCKING

(4.) Firing. Firing occurs when the firing pin strikes the primer. As the trigger is pulled the trigger lugs are disengaged from the hammer hooks and the hammer is released. The hammer moves forward under the pressure of the hammer spring and strikes the tang of the firing pin, driving the firing pin against the primer and firing the round (fig. 27).

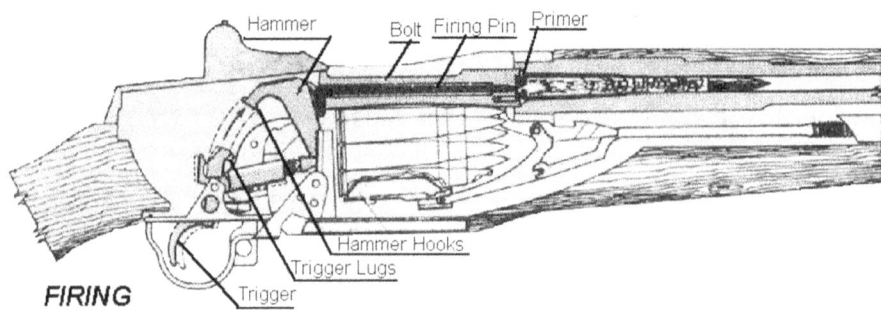
FIRING

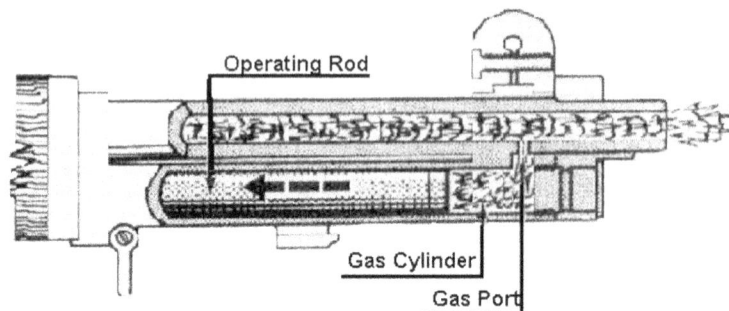
ACTION OF THE GAS

(5.) Unlocking. Unlocking occurs after the firing of the round. As the bullet is forced through the barrel by the expanding gas, a small portion of the gas escapes through the gas port into the gas cylinder, forcing the operating rod to the rear (fig. 28).

(6.) The camming surface inside the recess in the hump of the operating rod forces the operating lug of the bolt upward, disengaging the locking lugs from their recesses in the receiver. The bolt is thus unlocked and ready to be moved to the rear (fig. 29).

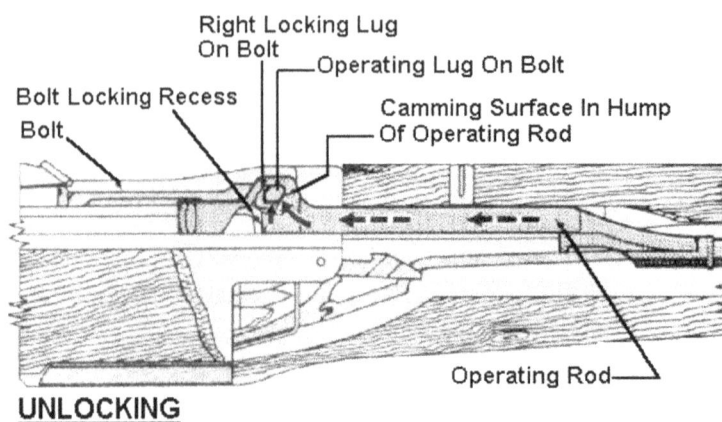
UNLOCKING

(6.) Extracting. Extracting is pulling the empty cartridge case from the chamber. The extractor, which is engaged with the extracting groove on the cartridge case, withdraws the empty case as the bolt moves to the rear (fig. 30).

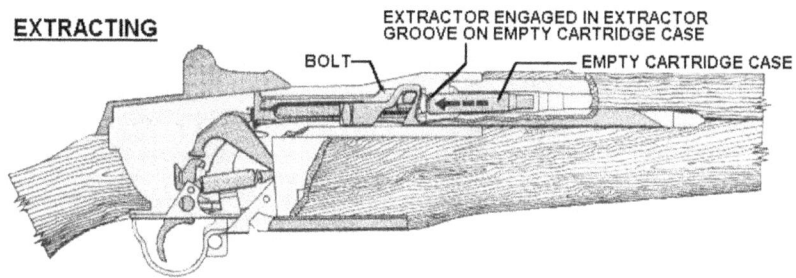

EXTRACTING

BOLT

EXTRACTOR ENGAGED IN EXTRACTOR
GROOVE ON EMPTY CARTRIDGE CASE

EMPTY CARTRIDGE CASE

(7.) Ejecting. Ejecting is throwing the empty case from the rifle. As the bolt moves to the rear, withdrawing the case from the chamber, the round is held in place by the chamber walls. When the mouth of the empty case clears the chamber, it is ejected up and to the right by the expanding ejector spring and ejector.

(8.) Cocking. Cocking occurs when the hammer is forced into the proper position for firing the next round. This happens as the bolt continues to the rear. The rear end of the bolt forces the hammer back and rides over it. The hammer is caught by the sear if the trigger is still held to the rear, but it is caught by the trigger lugs if trigger pressure has been released (fig. 31).

Chapter 4.

STOPPAGES AND IMMEDIATE ACTION

16. Stoppages

(a.) A stoppage is any unintentional interruption in the cycle of operation.

(b.) Most stoppages occur because of dirty, worn, or broken parts, and lack of lubrication. The rifleman must be taught to watch for these defects and take corrective action to eliminate them before they cause a stoppage. Some of the more common stoppages, with their usual causes and remedies are shown in table.

17. Immediate Action

(a.) Immediate action is the prompt action taken by the firer to reduce a stoppage. To apply immediate action, pull the operating rod handle all the way to the rear with the right hand, *palm up*, then release it. The right hand should be held in this manner so it will not be injured in the event of a hangfire. Next, aim the rifle and try to fire it.

(b.) If a rifleman is taught to apply immediate action quickly and properly when his rifle fails to fire, he will be able to reduce most stoppages

18. Misfire, Hangfire, and Cookoff

(a.) Hangfires and misfires rarely occur. Normally, the firer will instinctively apply immediate action which in most instances reduces the stoppage even when caused by a hangfire or misfire.

(b.) Misfires are caused by one of three factors - the firer, the weapon malfunctioning (due to excessive dirt, etc.), or faulty ammunition. When there has been an excessive number of misfires caused by faulty ammunition, the lot number should be reported to ammunition supply personnel for inspection and determination of disposition.

19. Malfunction

A malfunction is a failure of the weapon to operate satisfactorily. Some of the common malfunctions are discussed below.

(a.) The clip may jump out on the seventh round. This is usually caused by a bent follower arm or bullet guide and can be corrected by replacing them.'

(b.) The rifle may fire in bursts of two or three rounds. This is due to the sear being broken, worn, or remaining in an open position. It can be corrected by replacing the trigger assembly.

(c.) The safety may release when pressure is applied to the trigger. This can be caused by a broken safety or by the trigger stop on the safety being worn. It can be corrected by replacing the safety.

Table II.
Stoppages, Their Causes and Remedies

STOPPAGES	CAUSES	REMEDY
Failure to feed	Lack of lubrication of operating parts	Clean and lubricate operating parts
"	Defective or worn parts	Replace parts
"	Short recoil	See paragraph 19 (Malfunction) Section (d.)
Failure to chamber	Lack of lubrication of operating parts	Clean and lubricate operating parts
	Dirty chamber	Clean chamber
Failure to lock	Lack of lubrication of operating parts	Clean and lubricate operating parts
"	Dirty chamber	Clean chamber
"	Dirty locking recesses	Clean recesses
"	Weak operating rod spring	Replace spring
Failure to fire	Defective ammunition	Replace ammunition
"	Defective firing pin	Replace firing pin Replace trigger housing group
"	Defective trigger housing group	Replace trigger housing group
Failure to unlock	Dirty chamber	Clean chamber
"	Lack of lubrication of operating parts	Clean and lubricate operating parts
"	Insufficient gas	Tighten gas cylinder lock screw. Clean or replace worn parts
Failure to extract	Dirty chamber	Clean chamber
"	Dirty ammunition	Replace ammunition
"	Broken extractor	Replace extractor
Failure to eject	Broken ejector spring	Replace ejector or spring
"	Short recoil	See paragraph 19 (Malfunction) Section (d.)
Failure to cock	Defective trigger housing group	Replace trigger housing group
"	Short recoil	See paragraph 19 (Malfunction) Section (d.)

Chapter 5.

MAINTENANCE

20. General

Maintenance includes all measures taken to keep the rifle in operating condition. This includes normal cleaning, inspection for defective parts, repair, and lubrication.

21. Cleaning, Materials, Lubricants, and Equipment.

(a.) Cleaning Materials.

(1.) Bore cleaner (cleaning compound solvent (CR)) is used primarily for cleaning the bore; however, it may be used on all metal parts for temporary (1-day) protection from rust.

(2.) Hot, soapy water or boiling water is no substitute for bore cleaner and will only be used when bore cleaner is not available.

(3.) Dry cleaning solvent is used for cleaning rifles which are coated with grease, oil, or corrosion-preventative compounds.

(4.) Stubborn carbon deposits are removed by soaking in carbon removing compound (PCIII-A) and brushing. This process must be followed by the use of drycleaning solvent.

Caution: Individual protective measures must be taken when using compound PCIII-A.

(b.) Lubricants.

(1.) Lubricating oil, general purpose (PL special) is used for lubricating the rifle at normal temeratures.

(2.) Lubricating oil, weapons (LAW) is used for low temperatures (below 0 degrees).

(3.) OE 10 engine oil may be used as a field expedient under combat conditons when the oils prescribed in (1.) and (2.) above cannot be obtained. However, the weapon should be cleaned and lubricated with the proper lubricants as soon as possible

(4.) Rifle grease should be applied to those working surfaces as shown in figure 33.

(c.) Equipment.

A complete set of maintenance equipment (figure 34) and (figure 35) is stored in the stocks of the M1 and M1C rifles and consists of:

M10 cleaning rod (4 sections with handle and plastic buffer).

Small arms bore cleaning brush.

Lubrication case.

Chamber cleaning brush. (NOTE: Insure the M1 chamber brush is used. The M14 rifle chamber brush is 1/2-inch shorter and will not clean the M1 chamber).

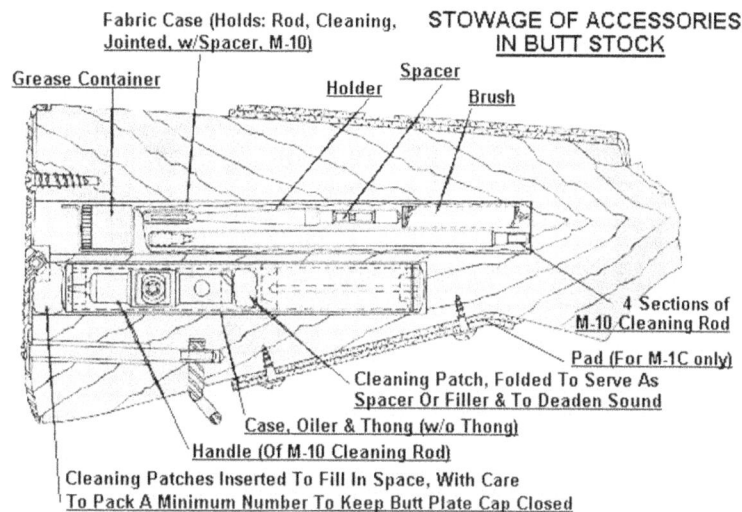

Fabric Case (Holds: Rod, Cleaning, Jointed, w/Spacer, M-10) STOWAGE OF ACCESSORIES IN BUTT STOCK

Grease Container

Spacer

Holder

Brush

4 Sections of M-10 Cleaning Rod

Pad (For M-1C only)

Cleaning Patch, Folded To Serve As Spacer Or Filler & To Deaden Sound

Case, Oiler & Thong (w/o Thong)

Handle (Of M-10 Cleaning Rod)

Cleaning Patches Inserted To Fill In Space, With Care To Pack A Minimum Number To Keep Butt Plate Cap Closed

22. Cleaning the Rifle

(a.) The rifle must be cleaned after it has been fired because firing produces primer fouling, powder ashes, carbon, and metal fouling. The ammunition now manufactured has a noncorrosive primer which makes cleaning easier, but no less important. The primer still leaves a deposit that may collect moisture and promote rust if it is not removed. The cleaning described below will remove all deposits except metal fouling which is relatively uncommon and is removed by maintenance personnel.

(1.) Chamber. Remove the patch holder from the cleaning rod and insert two patches about halfway through the slot. Dip the patches in bore cleaner, then wring or squeeze the excess fluid from the patches. Screw the M10 cleaning rod together (less the patch holder) and insert it all the way into the bore. Flare the patches out, then insert the patch holder with the wet patches into the chamber. Push the threaded end into the chamber until it touches the cleaning rod. Hold it there with one hand and screw the cleaning rod and the patch holder together. Pull the patches to the chamber; at the same time turning the rod clockwise. Turn the rod several times, wiping the chamber thoroughly. After the chamber has been thoroughly cleaned use the chamber brush in the following manner:

(a) Screw a section of the M10 cleaning rod into a threaded hole of the driver ratchet.

(b) Place the brush into the chamber of the barrel.

(c) Allow the rifle bolt to close slowly against the end of the driver ratchet.

(d) Using the rod section as a handle, rotate the driver clockwise and counter-clockwise to loosen and clean residue from the chamber.

(2) Bore. To clean the bore saturate the bore brush with cleaning compound solvent (rifle bore cleaner) and -

(a) Insert the bore brush into the chamber. Insert the cleaning rod into the bore and screw the brush onto the rod.

(b) Pull the brush through the bore. Remove the brush and repeat the procedure as often as required to clean the bore.

(c) Then use one cleaning patch dampened with bore cleaner in the following manner:

Place the patch in the patch holder and insert it into the chamber.

Insert the cleaning rod (less the patch holder) into the bore and screw it onto the patch holder.

Pull the cleaning rod through the bore. Repeat this procedure using as many patches as required until the patches come through the bore clean.

(3) Gas cylinder lock screw with valve assembly. Remove carbon deposits by using bore cleaner, then wipe the part and oil it lightly (do not use abrasives). Check the valve to see that it is not held open by particles of dirt or sand.

(4) Piston of operating rod. Remove carbon from the piston with bore cleaner. Take care not to damage the piston. Oil it lightly after cleaning (do not use abrasives).

(5) Gas Cylinder. Clean the gas cylinder with bore cleaner and with patches.

(6) Face of the bolt. Clean the face of the bolt with a patch and bore cleaner, paying particular attention to its inside edges. Remove the bore cleaner with dry patches and oil the part lightly.

(7) All other parts. Use a dry cloth to remove all dirt or sand from other parts and exterior surfaces. Apply a light coat of oil to the metal parts and rub raw linseed oil into the wooden parts. Care must be taken to prevent linseed oil from getting on metal parts.

(8) Cleaning frequency. The rifle must be thoroughly cleaned no later than the evening of the day it is fired. For three consecutive days thereafter check for evidence of fouling by running a clean patch through the bore and inspecting it. The bore should be lightly oiled after each inspection.

23. Normal Maintenance

(a.) When in use, the rifle should be inspected daily for evidence of rust and general appearance. A light coat of oil (PL Special) should be maintained on metal parts.

(b.) The daily inspection should also reveal any defects such as burred, worn, or cracked parts. Defects should be reported to the armorer for correction.

(c.) A muzzle plug should never be used on the rifle. It causes moisture to collect in the bore, which causes bore rust that is a safety hazard.

(d.) Obtaining the proper rear sight tension is extremely important; without it the sight will not hold its adjustment in elevation. During normal maintenance and prior to firing, the rear sight must be checked for correct sight tension. The indications of improper sight tension are: elevation knob extremely difficult to turn, and elevation knob turn freely without an audible click.

(1) If the elevation knob is extremely difficult to turn, the soldier must rotate the windage knob nut (with the scew-driver portion of the M10 cleaning rod handle) counterclockwise one click at a time. After each click an attempt should be made to turn the elevation knob. Repeat this process until the elevation knob can be turned without extreme difficulty.

(2) In the event the elevation knob is extremely loose and the rear sight aperture will not raise, the windage knob nut must be turned in a clockwise direction, one click at a time, until the aperture can be raised.

(3) To check for proper tension the procedures listed below should be followed:

(a) Raise the aperture to its full height.

(b) Lower the aperture two clicks.

(c) Grasp the rifle with the fingers around the small of the stock and exert downward pressure on the aperture with the thumb of the same hand.

(4) If the aperture drops, sight tension must be adjusted. To do this the windage knob nut must be turned in a clockwise direction one click at a time until the aperture can no longer be pushed down. If the proper tension cannot be obtained, the rifle must be turned in to the unit armorer.

24. Special Maintenance

(a.) Before firing the rifle, the bore and the chamber should be cleaned and dried. A light coat of oil should be placed on all other metal parts except those which come in contact with ammunition.

(b.) Before firing, rifle grease should be applied to the parts indicated in figure 33. A small amount of grease is taken up on the stem of the grease container cap and is applied at each place. Rifle grease is not used in extremely cold temperatures or when the rifle is exposed to extremes of sand

and dust.

      (c.) In cold climates (temperatures below freezing) the rifle must be kept free of moisture and excess oil. Moisture and excess oil on the working parts cause them to operate sluggishly or fail completely. The rifles must be disassembled and wiped with a clean, dry cloth. Drycleaning solvent may be used if necessary to remove oil or grease. Parts that show signs of wear may be wiped with a patch lightly dampened with lubricating oil (LAW). It is best to keep the rifle as close as possible to outside temperatures at all times to prevent the collection of moisture which occurs when cold metal comes in contact with warm air. When the rifle is brought into a warm room, it should not be cleaned until it has reached room temperature.

(d.) In hot, humid climates or if exposed to salt water or salt-water atmosphere, the rifle must be inspected thoroughly each day for signs of moisture and rust. It should be kept lightly oiled with special preservative lubricating oil. Raw linseed oil should be applied frequently to the wooden parts to prevent swelling.

(e.) In hot, dry climates the rifle must be cleaned daily or more often to remove sand and/or dust from the bore and working parts. In sandy areas, the rifle should be kept dry. The muzzle and receiver should be kept covered during sand and dust storms. Wooden parts must be kept oiled with raw linseed oil to prevent drying. The rifle should be lightly oiled when sandy or dusty conditions decrease.

(f.) Special instructions on caring for the rifle when it is subject to nuclear, biological, or chemical contamination can be found in TM 3-220 and FM-21-40.

Rifle, U.S. Caliber .30, M1 (GARAND)

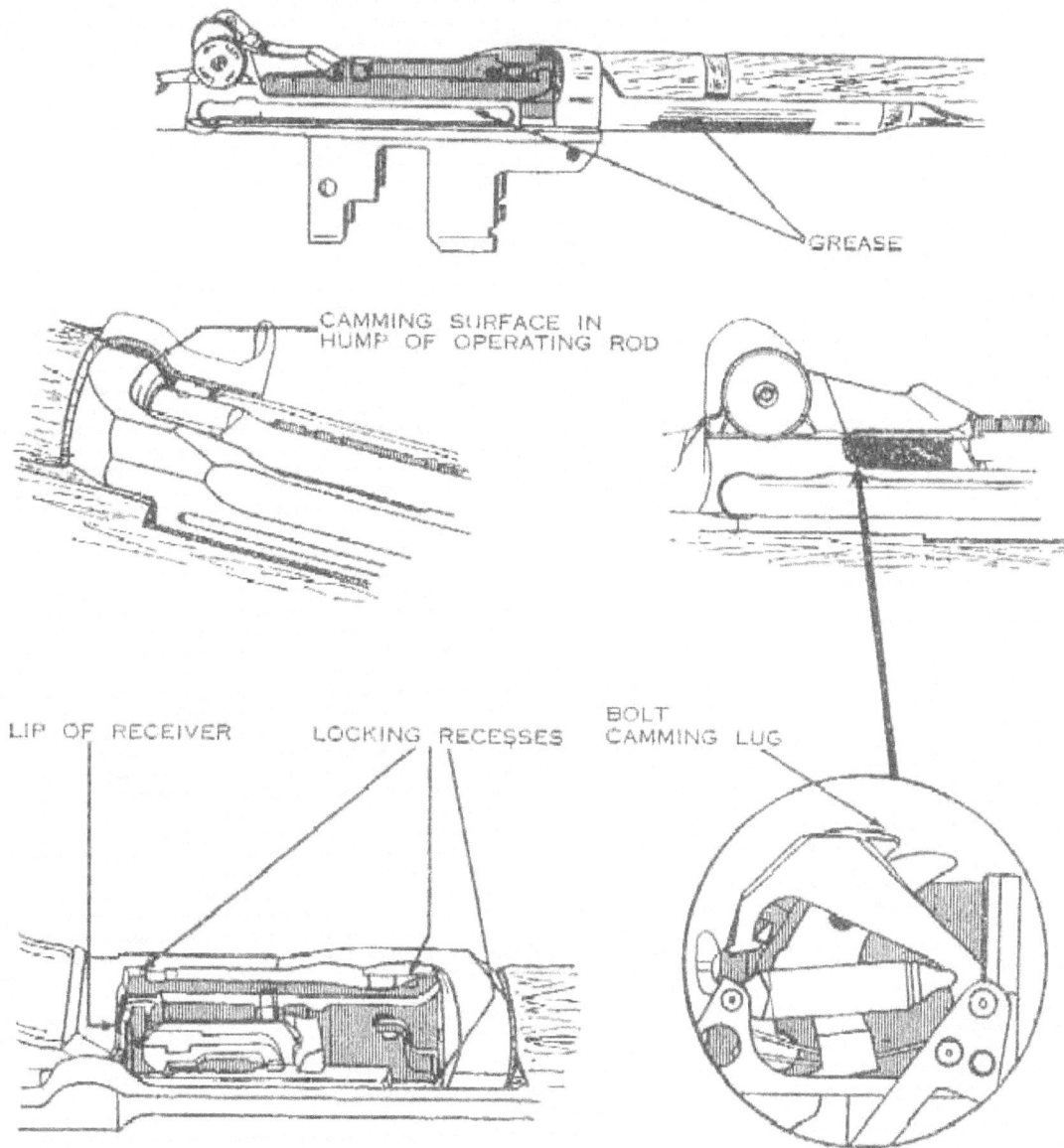

GREASE

CAMMING SURFACE IN
HUMP OF OPERATING ROD

LIP OF RECEIVER   LOCKING RECESSES   BOLT
                                                  CAMMING LUG

Points to Apply Rifle Grease on the M1 Garand

Chapter 6.

AMMUNITION

25. General

The M1 rifle fires several types of ammunition. The rifleman should be able to recognize them and know which type is best for certain targets. The M1, M1C and M1D Garand rifles fire .30 U.S. (.30-06) ammunition. Commercial sporting type ammunition will usually function if the bullets are of the right length, and are loaded to pressures approximating those of military loads. When using other than military issue ammunition, the sights (peep or scope) must be zeroed in for various ranges with the particular type of ammunition, due to differences in velocities and wind-bucking characteristics of the particular round. Military ammunition is marked on the tip of the bullet in color, indicating the type of bullet.

26. Description

a. Ball, M-2. This cartridge is used against personnel and unarmored targets, and can be identified by its unpainted bullet. M-2 ball is the most common of the military loads, is not marked in color, as it is the only one left plain (aside from the frangible ball). It has a gilding-metal jacket. The length of the bullet is 1.123 inches

b. Armor Piercing, M-2. This cartridge is used against lightly armored vehicles, protective shelters, and personnel, and can be identified by its black bullet tip.

c. Armor Piercing Incendiary, M-14. This cartridge is used, in place of the armor piercing round, against flammable targets. The tip of the bullet is colored with aluminum or white paint.

d. Incendiary, M-1. This cartridge is used against unarmored, flammable targets. The tip of the bullet is painted blue.

e. Tracers and M-25. These cartridges are for use in observing fire, signaling, target designation, and incendiary purposes. The tips of the bullets are painted red for the M1 and orange for the M25.

f. Blank, M-1909. This cartridge is used to simulate rifle fire, firing salutes, training and signaling. The cartridge is identified by having no bullet, and by the cannelure in the neck of the case which is sealed by red lacquer.

g. Rifle Grenade Cartridge, M-3. This cartridge is used with the grenade launcher to propel grenades. The cartridge has no bullet and the mouth is crimped.

h. Dummy, M-40. This cartridge is used for mechanical training. These are two types. One has longitudal grooves in the case, and is usually tin plated. Another merely has small holes in the case, and no primer. These are also of use on the range when mixed in with a clip of ammo, to detect flinching on the part of the firer.

i. Match. This cartridge, used in marksmanship competition firing, can be identified by the word "MATCH" on the head stamp.

j. Frangible ball M-22. This cartridge is unmarked, but is identifiable by its bullet length, which is 1.185 inches (as opposed to 1.123 for M-2 ball).

The approximate maximum range and average muzzle velocity of the .30 caliber ammunition issued for the M1, M1C and M1D rifles is:

Cartridge	Maximum Range (yds)	Feet Per Second
Ball, M-2	3500	2800
Tracer, M-1	3350	2750
Incendiary, M-1	2875	3020
Armor-piercing, M-2	3160	2770
Armor Piercing Incendiary M-14	3300	2830

Ammunition for the .30 M1 series of rifles usually comes packed in eight-round clips, which in turn are packed in bandoleers, and in metal cans. Ammunition may also come packed in 20-round boxes.

The standard means for carrying ammunition for the M1 was in the cartridge belt. The M1923 cartridge belt adopted for use with the M1903 Springfield rifle and its five round chargers was the belt originally issued with the M1. This belt had ten pockets which could hold either two 5 round '03 chargers or one eight round M1 clip each. After the adoption of the M1, the Model 1938 cartridge belt was adopted. This belt was essentially identical to the earlier M1923 belt but had twelve pockets instead of ten to provide extra ammunition for the greater firepower of the M1.

MIDDLE
COAST
PUBLISHING

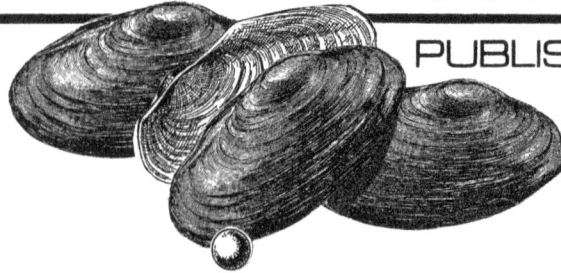

Middle-Coast-Publishing.com

On the following pages is a catalog of our Military Firearms Series of Books, all of which are available at Amazon Books.

FREDERIC FAUST

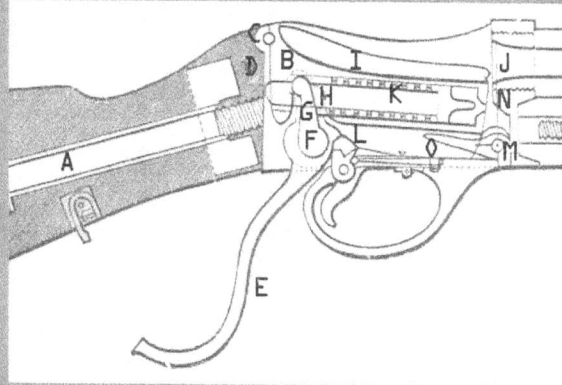

The Lineage of the Martini-Henry Rifle

Facts and Circumstances in the History and Development of the Martini-Henry Rifle

ISBN-13: 978-0934523-56-1

The Martini–Henry breech-loading single-shot lever-actuated rifle, entered British Army service in 1871. Martini–Henry variants, used throughout the British Empire for 30 years, combined the dropping-block action first developed by Henry O. Peabody (in his Peabody rifle) and improved by the Swiss designer Friedrich von Martini, combined with the polygonal barrel rifling designed by Scotsman Alexander Henry. Find out the details on exactly how these rifles work and who was Martini and who was Henry.

K RIFLE MK

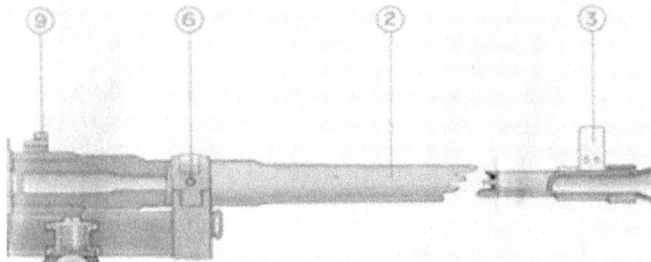

ARMOURER'S NOTES:
BOYS ANTI-TANK RIFLE
With
Parts Listing and Diagrams

8	PISTOL GRIP.		11	SHOULDER PIECE.
9	BACKSIGHT BRACKET AND BACKSIGHT.		12	SHOULDER PIECE GRIP.
10	CHEEK REST.		13	OIL BOTTLE.

ISBN: 97809344523-6-46

Armourer's Notes: Boys Anti-tank Rifle explains to troops how to employ and maintain the Boys Anti-Tank Rifle. Coverage includes a breakdown of the weapon by salient groups, showing a diagram of each individual parts and identifying those parts by name and stock number.

LEE-ENFIELD

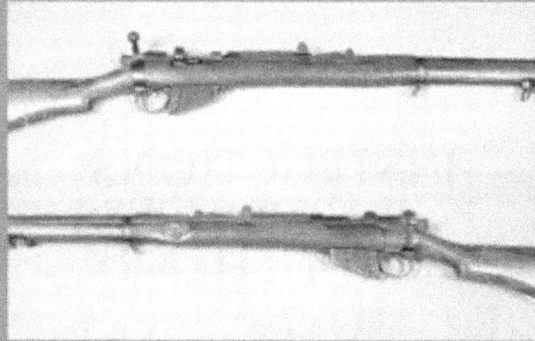

INSTRUCTIONS FOR ARMOURERS

Rifles No. 1, No. 2, and Rifle No. 3 (Pattern 14)

ISBN-13: 978-0934523-11-0

British War Office notes, circa 1931, on the SMLE provide unit armourers with detailed information on how to: Strip and reassemble the bolt and magazine; Clean a rusty barrel, Clear an obstructed bore, Check headspace, Replace a bolt head, Adjust trigger pull, Troubleshoot misfires, Fit a new striker, Blacking sights, and Fit a new fore end.

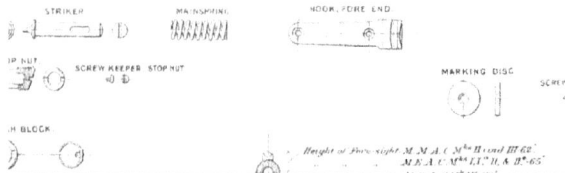

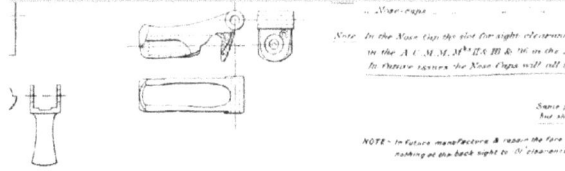

ISBN-13: 978-0934523-55-4

Get genuine Martini-Henry gunsmithing techniques from the primary source, the British Army, circa 1897. This armourer's text tells exactly how to maintain and care for your rifle, from assembly and disassembly to simple fixes to the breech block and trigger.

LEE-ENFIELD RIFLE
EXPLODED DRAWINGS
AND PARTS LISTS

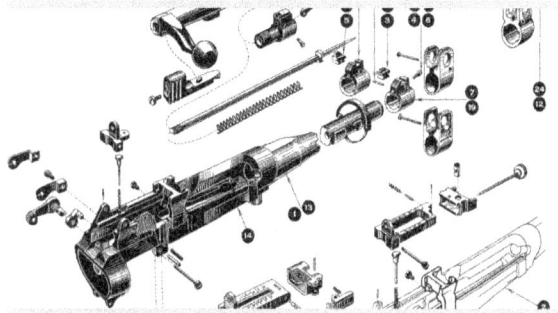

RIFLES NO. 1 MARK III (SMLE) - NO. 3 (PATTERN 14) - NO. 4 MARKS I & MARKI*

FREDERIC FAUST

ISBN-13: 978-0934523-63-9

This copiously illustrated Reprint of a 1945 War Department document shows each rifle by way of exploded drawings of the main components and sub-assemblies. Each part is identified by name and number. Published in large format (8 X 10).

LEE-ENFIELD RIFLE NO. 4 MARK I*

PHANTOM PARTS DIAGRAMS AND PARTS LISTING

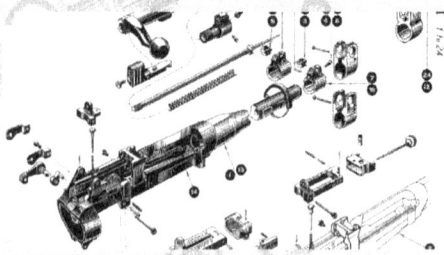

FREDERIC FAUST

ISBN-13: 978-0934523-65-3

Built at the Canadian Long Branch Arsenal many aficionados consider the old warhorse to be the best of all the variants fielded during the Second World War. This book contains parts identification lists detailing by illustration, descriptive part name and part number, for all parts of the Rifle, .303 Calibre, Lee -Enfield, No 4, Mark 1 * and its associated equipment including bayonet, frog, action cover, wire gauze and pull-through. Parts are listed to show major assemblies, sub-assemblies, and component parts.

DEPARTMENT OF THE ARMY

FM 23-5

U.S. Rifle Caliber .30 M1

ISBN: 978-0934523-09-7

Profusely illustrated, this Department of the Army **REPRINT** is a guide in the instruction and training in the mechanical operation of the M1 Garand rifle, once described by General George S Patton as The Greatest Battle Implement ever devised. Coverage includes detailed description of the rifle, general characteristics; procedures for disassembly and assembly; methods of loading; an explanation of functioning; a discussion of stoppages and immediate action; a description of the ammunition; and instructions on the care and cleaning of both the weapon and ammunition.

Ordnance Field Service Manual

RIGHT BIPOD LEG GROUP
LEFT BIPOD LEG ASSY
16, 57

Browning
M1918A2

Rifle, Auto, Caliber .30 Browning

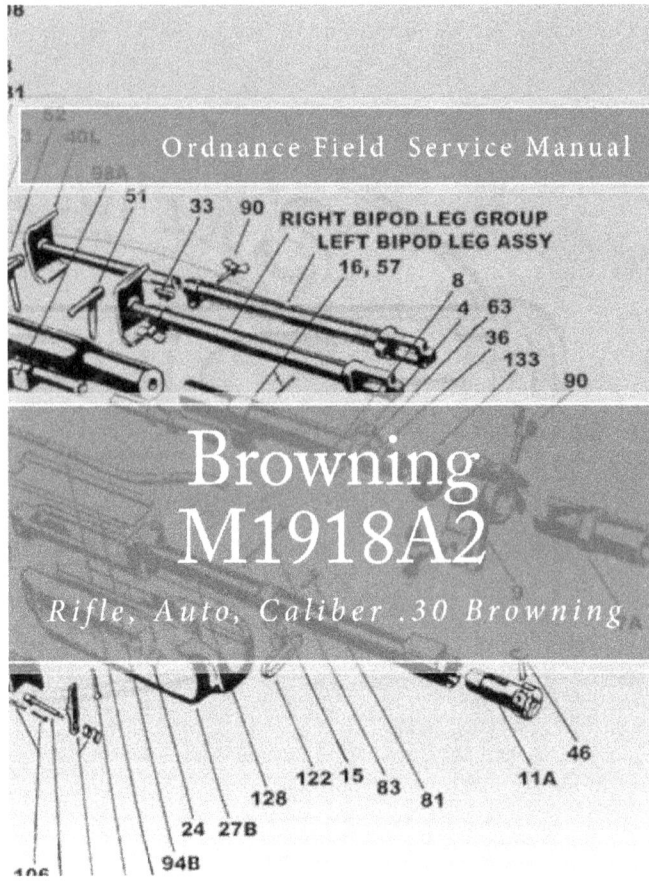

ISBN-13: 978-1541187-51-1

This comprehensive, large format reprint of a Rock Island Arsenal manual shows by way of phantom drawings all of the venerable BAR's parts and how they fit together.

U.S ARMY TECHNICAL MANUAL Type 99 Arisaka Caliber .30

Korean War Reprint
Colonel Arisaka Nakiakiara

ISBN: 978-0934523-68-4

During the Korean War, approximately 126,500 short and 6,650 long Type 99 Rifles were re-chambered under American supervision at the Tokyo arsenal to fire the U.S. Military M2 -.30-06 Springfield cartridge. These rifles were fitted with a lengthened magazine well and had a small notch cut in the top of the receiver ring in order to accommodate the .30-06 round's 1/3 of an inch greater overall length. The Pentagon rather wisely wrote a Technical Manual for the converted rifles that addresses inspection of the weapon, care, assembly and function. This then is that TM.

FREDERIC FAUST

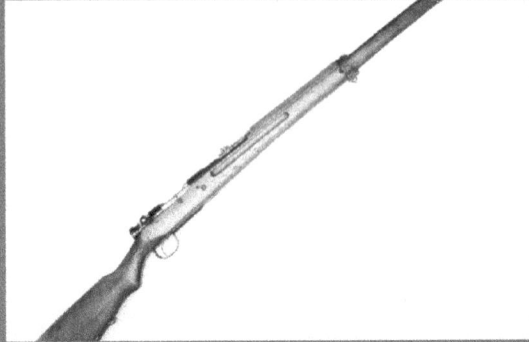

The Lineage of the Arisaka

Facts and Circumstance in the History of the Arisaka Family of Rifles

ISBN: 978-0934523-32-5

The Arisaka family of Japanese military bolt-action service rifles, in production and use from 1897 until the end of World War II in 1945. The most common specimens include the Type 38 chambered for the 6.5×50mmSR Type 38 cartridge and the Type 99 chambered for the 7.7×58mm Type 99 cartridge. Many thousands of Type 99s and other Arisaka variants were brought to the United States by soldiers as war trophies during and after World War II. Find out about the rifle's namesake Colonel Arisaka and learn the fascinating history of this esteemed battle rifle.

EDITED BY FREDERIC FAUST

The Lineage of the Lee-Enfield Rifle

Facts and Circumstance in the
History of the .303 British

ISBN-13: 978-0934523-30-1

This book chronicles the history and development of the family of the venerable Lee-Enfield rifle, beginning in 1895 with a redesign of the Lee-Metford. On its pages you'll learn what an SMLE is and what is not, find out which countries carried it and which wars it fought in plus consult the registry of serial numbers for Rifles No. 4 and No. 5.

FREDERIC FAUST

The Lineage of the Mosin-Nagant

Facts and Circumstance in the History & Development of this Battle Rifle

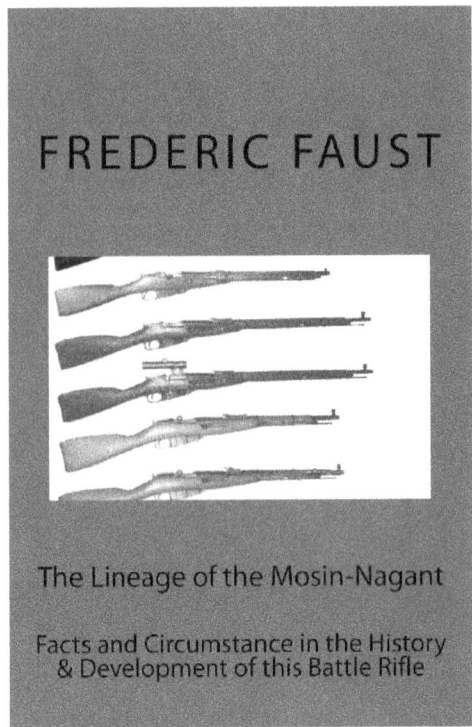

ISBN-13: 978-0934523-15-8

The Mosin–Nagant is a five-shot, bolt-action, internal magazine-fed, military rifle, developed by the Imperial Russian Army in 1882–91 and used by the armed forces of the Russian Empire, the Soviet Union and various other nations.

It is one of the most mass-produced military bolt-action rifles in history with over 37 million units produced since its invention in 1891. And in spite of its age, it has pulled duty in various armed conflicts around the world even up to the modern day. This comes as no big surprise when considering how these rifles are plentiful, cheap, rugged, simple to use, and effective, much like the AK-47 and its variants.

Find out about the parts played by the rifles namesakes Mosin and Nagant. Learn all about the fascinating history and evolution of this esteemed battle rifle.

www.ingramcontent.com/pod-product-compliance
Lightning Source LLC
Chambersburg PA
CBHW081232020426
42331CB00012B/3144